1450-1

Praise for 1959 edition of *1450-1950*:

"I have enjoyed myself enormously, in every way enormously."

~Gertrude Stein

"And I like it immensely."

~Marcel Duchamp

"I hear that that compendium of insanely sensible 'painfully hand-lettered' poems (or is it a delightfully impressive mad drawing, conceived during a masculine pregnancy?) yclept *1450-1950* is about to be republished. Thank God, and GOODY, GOODY; believe it or not!"

~Carl Van Vechten

"You rise like a ghost come to life from the legion of the vanished . . . I am one of the few who is sure you are not more bughouse than Rabelais or William Blake. I have read the book silently and then out loud in a family circle. There is life in the old hoss yet . . ."

~Carl Sandburg

"Bookshelves are deficient in laughs. Everyone is so busy being a Brain they are content mostly to leave Aristophanes in the hands of anybody who has nothing better to do than smile. So when you just burst out laughing and can't get the sound of it down on the typewriter or find it in any other book read *THE FROGS* or Bob Brown's *1450-1950* with pictures, hand-hewn by the author himself."

~Walter Lowenfels

"How many?
Why not? You should.
'—intelligent et jeune
Comme l'avenir,
Comme le rire!'"

~James Johnson Sweeney

"It is the most original book I have read except *The Life and Romance of an Algebraist*."

~Gelett Burgess

"The years 1928-29 in Paris were a great time for me. One of the contributing factors was my close friendship with Bob Brown while he was getting 1450-1950 into shape. He achieved a classic architecture for the transference of casual good will in this process. I look forward to the republication of his unique and true book to serve a like function in my current euphoric method."

~Stuart Davis

"We show your book to everyone who comes to the house and they always find some page that so especially delights them that soon we will have to chain it down like an ancient missal."

~Caresse Crosby

Praise for 2015 edition:

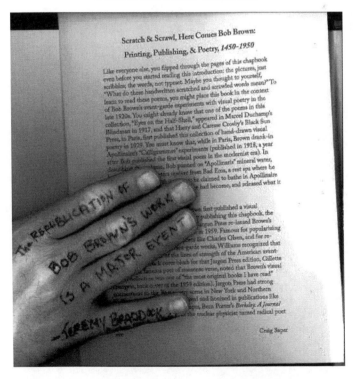

1450-1950

Other titles by Roving Eye Press

The Readies
Words
Gems: A Censored Anthology

These works are available for free download on the Roving Eye Press website.

Other titles by Bob Brown

The Remarkable Adventures of Christopher Poe
What Happened to Mary
Tahiti : 10 Rhythms
My Marjonary
Globe-Gliding
Demonics
Nomadness
Readies for Bob Brown's Machine
Let There Be Beer!
Houdini
Homemade Hilarity
Can We Co-Operate?
The Complete Book of Cheese
14 Poets, 1 Artist

(with Rose & Cora Brown)
The European Cookbook for American Homes
10,000 Snacks
The Country Cookbook
Salads and Herbs
The Vegetable Cook Book
Most for Your Money Cookbook
Outdoor Cooking
The South American Cook Book

1450-1950
by Bob Brown

Edited with and Introduction by Craig Saper

"Eyes of Globe," Courtesy of Charles Bernstein.

www.rovingeyepress.com

First published by Roving Eye Press, 2015

ISBN 10: 0692432469
ISBN 13: 9780692432464

Cover Design: Bob Brown, Lynn Tomlinson, & K. A. Wisniewski
Book Layout and Typesetting: K. A. Wisniewski

Special thanks to Jonathan Williams (1929-2008) for his permissions to
reprint the Jargon Press edition and his efforts to keep this title in print.

Table of Contents

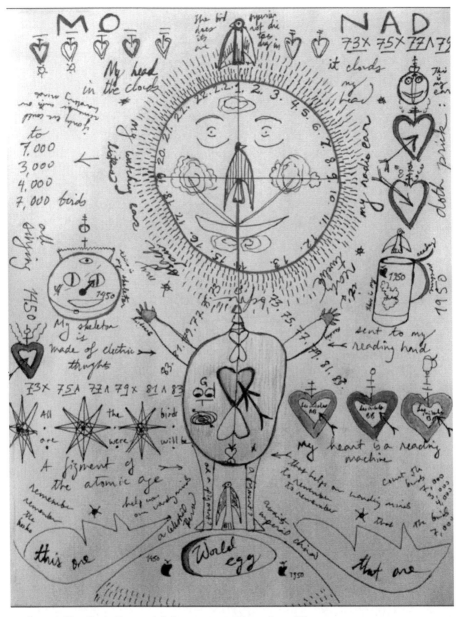

"Monad (for Bob Brown)," Courtesy of Jonathan Eburne.

Scratch & Scrawl, Here Comes Bob Brown:

Printing, Publishing, & Poetry, *1450-1950*

Like everyone else, you flipped through the pages of this chapbook even before you started reading this introduction: the pictures, just scribbles; the words, not typeset. Maybe you thought to yourself, "What do these handwritten scratched and scrawled words mean?" To learn to read these poems, you might place this book in the context of Bob Brown's avant-garde experiments with visual poetry in the late 1920s. You might already know that one of the poems in this collection, "Eyes on the Half-Shell," appeared in Marcel Duchamp's Blindman in 1917, and that Harry and Caresse Crosby's Black Sun Press, in Paris, first published this collection of hand-drawn visual poetry in 1929. You must know that, while in Paris, Brown drank-in Apollinaire's "Calligrammes" experiments (published in 1918, a year after Bob published the first visual poem in the modernist era). In describing this volume, Bob punned on "Apollinaris" mineral water, bottled eighty kilometers upriver from Bad Ems, a rest spa where he went after publishing this volume: he claimed to bathe in Apollinaire as part of the cure for what literature had become, and released what it could become.

More than half a century after Brown first published a visual poem, and nearly three decades after publishing this chapbook, the publisher-poet, Jonathan Williams' Jargon Press re-issued Brown's collection to an American audience in 1959. Famous for popularizing the Black Mountain College poets like Charles Olson, and for re-issuing less well-known avant-garde works, Williams recognized that Bob Brown "was one of the lines of strength of the American avant-garde." On the back cover blurb for that Jargon Press edition, Gillette Burgess, the famous poet of nonsense verse, noted that Brown's visual poetry collection was one of "the most original books I have read" (Burgess, back cover of the 1959 edition). Jargon Press had strong connections to the Beat poetry scene in New York and Northern California. Brown was interviewed and lionized in publications like the tabloid-style culture newspaper, Bern Porter's *Berkeley: A Journal of Modern Culture*. Porter was the nuclear physicist turned radical poet

Craig Saper

that embodied politics of resistance and the reemergence of a counter-cultural poetry. These poets and artists looked to the then little known expatriate avant-garde of the 1920s as lineage and models. These various groups started to reissue and publish reports on leaders of the expatriate avant-garde, like the report Bob Brown wrote on Gertrude Stein and her circle. And new editions of these alternative poetries were published. In Brazil, Augusto de Campos published an edition of *1450-1950* in the early 1960s. Dick Higgins' Something Else Press and the Fluxus group began publishing their own poetry experiments alongside these expatriate works especially works of "concrete" and visual poetry. After another more than half a century hiatus, Brown's works have now begun to reappear as his works speak to our contemporary concerns about new forms of poetry (LANGUAGE poetry, Conceptual Poetry, etc.). Also, the interest in the ways that electronic machines impact reading have drawn considerable scholarly interest to Brown's work in areas like "digital modernism," and from those looking for analogies to electronic literature. Brown includes a readie as the first poem in this collection. The newly re-started Roving Eye Press has also published Brown's *Words*, *The Readies*, and *Gems*.

One of the poems in this collection offers in a *mise-en-abyme* another context to read this entire collection of poems and all of Brown's life and career; Bob Brown's own self-portrait as visual poem functions as a schematic map to reading this volume. The handwritten captions on different parts of his stick-figure include references to poems in this volume, like "My Skeleton Both Articulates and Gesticulates," and, again, in *mise-en-abyme* fashion, half of this book's title appears in the upper left hand corner, "1450," and the other half appears in the lower right corner, "1950." One handwritten tag, "my art," is scribbled over his heart; and that heart is a dingbat-like visual design that he used as the logo for this collection of visual poetry. Next to the logo-heart is "My Rose Rib," an allusion to Adam's rib and to Brown's partner and wife, Rose. In this same self-poem, or what we now might call a conceptual poem selfie, he includes a miniature of his entire "Eyes On The Half Shell," that shows the influence of Marcel Duchamp, a friend and mentor of Bob's before and during the years in France with the expatriate avant-garde. Brown turns his autobiographical sketch into a one of his characteristic comic visual poems that makes the abstracted shape an essential element of the meaning and self-conception. The optical aspect of these poems is of course crucial.

When you talk about modernist visual poetry, you start with Apollinaire's calligrams and cummings' manupictograms and typograms where the poet imbricates writing and illustration inextricably together. Of *1450-1950* Brown explains,

> I try to express myself through optical poems, as Apollinaire and cummings try, as I already tried in "Eyes on the Half Shell" in 1917, excited by the first 'Armory Show' and by the Tender Buttons of Gertrude Stein, excited by the combining of drawings and words. I don't believe that words by themselves are worth anything anymore, except when manipulated by artists (cummings and Boyle for example). I think that Coolidge (today: add Eisenhower) and Will Rogers exhausted them to the point that they were left without meaning, so pale and dirty as the cents that Rockefeller and Woolworth rub among themselves. I think we need words in motion, to be read by the reading machine, I think we need to recapture something of the healthy hieroglyphic writing, now that oratory is dead and that what rests of poetry that is still read aloud is vociferate to us by electronicsniks.

The book is handwritten through most of the book including its dedication:

Craig Saper

Among this eccentric list of writers, artists, printers, whole categories of artists and artisans, and even a fictional murderous clown from the opera Pagliacci, Brown includes "MYSELF," and stresses in the visual form of the all-caps-handwritten list and in the whacky allusions, his own mix of visual and clowning elements that this collection embodies: Brown invents a type of slap-stick poetic burlesque. Calling it visual poetry is too staid and decorous; call it scratch & scrawl. If sonnets have a singular form and unvarying constraints for each and every instantiation, then scratch & scrawl depends on the absolutely particular trace, passions, and imperfection of the handwriting. The play between words and images shifts from a poetic tension to a conceptual game in which hand-drawn scribbles and pictures— blurring the boundaries between literal scribbles and conceptual poetry, it is difficult to describe them as one would a single medium like painting or film. Instead, the process of reading *1450-1950* follows an intimate discovery of a literally marginalized poetry (since the invention of the printing press). This collection is an extension of Gutenberg's creative legacy, a resistance to the standardized lines of type set, and the hilarious enervation of poetry's secret life usually under erasure by setting it in type – ALL OF THOSE CONFLICTING GOALS AT ONCE. It is scratch & scrawl: a next great poetry always already on the read page, but here it's a message in a bottle-booked-bound from a book-legger bobbed browned.

For this new 2015 edition, we invited a very few poets, artists, and scholars to riff on Brown's poetry, and they have in their own poetic ways answered that call. We could read these new contributions as homage, as specific riffs from contemporary branches in the conceptual-visual-poetry that Brown was working on about a hundred years before, or as speculative poetry on the future of what Bob Brown might call "readies," or simply the future of reading. Anna Banana, a founder and leader of the mail-art and stamp-art movement and a "conceptualist," contributed two works, "Homage to Bob Brown" AND "Roving Hand," that reference both her own roving hands and banana logic, and Brown's roving eye. Charles Bernstein, one of the founders and leaders of the LANGUAGE poetry movement as well as an important contemporary visual poet, contributed two poems as well, one of which, "Eyes on Globe," included here, and the other piece a GIF poem is available online at the Roving Eye Press website:

www.rovingeyepress.com. Amaranth Borsuk, one of the innovators
in the contemporary e-poetry movement with her works that explore
the ephemeral space between page and screen, contributed "A Healthy
Hieroglyphic," a reference to Brown's phrase of what's needed to
resuscitate writing, which is the QR-like-code-as-striking-image
on the last page of this introduction (and when holding the book
up to the screen at the poet's URL, a three-dimensional jumble of
Brownian words dances off the page). Jonathan Eburne, a major
scholar of surrealist and avant-garde writing, contributed "Monad (for
Bob Brown)," which is the frontispiece before this introduction. Kaja
Marczewska, a doctoral candidate writing about conceptual poetry
and "uncreative writing," sent "Look Before You Cook," which closes
this introductory chapter.

Although these biographical, literary, and cultural contexts help make
the reading more robust, there is something about this particular
collection that separates it even from those contexts: the handwriting
itself. The handwriting reinforces these poems improvisatory mood.
The short poems, never exceeding one page, and sometimes seemingly
two or three in one, also add to the immediacy and intimacy of these
poems. The readers feel like Bob is sitting next to them at the bar,
while drinking beers, as Bob draws these poems on a napkin as he
did in a bar with Marcel Duchamp. There is a sub-field of poetics
focused on visual poetry, but little of it studies the literary meaning of
handwriting. It is difficult to talk in general terms about something
so specific, something literally (and figuratively) not of "type," and
something that is rarely reproduced outside of the documentation of
an author's original notes. Of course, we knew it was crucial to publish
a facsimile edition of the poems because if one pours handwritten
poems into typography, the figures and figurative are lost, the oeuvre
and meaning erased. Although there is a rich semantic play in these
poems, there is no versifying formalism, no sign of any verse, not even
free or Imagist verse, which Brown had, many years earlier (in the
19-teens), parodied. *1450-1950* goes beyond parody, and calls for a
new poetics of scratch & scrawl.

Where do we begin to formulate a poetics of handwriting? For
Martin Heidegger, the hand, together with the word, distinguishes
human from animal, and the hand's script is handwriting. In that

Craig Saper

conception, handwriting is not peripheral, ornamental, or frivolous – it is the essence of the human. He goes on to discuss how the typewriter "degrades" and reduces the word down to a mere "means of communication" because type standardizes the word, the human character impressed in handwriting. "The typewriter makes everyone look the same." Later Jacques Derrida would recover the typewriter as something more, and other, than a standardization-and-reduction machine as typewriter-poets demonstrated. And, Avital Ronell would take dictation out of Heidegger's closet in a similar de-sedimentation as re-mixers and sound-poets have performed.

The discussion is beyond the scope of this introduction, but mentioning the importance of handwriting in philosophical and theoretical debates, helps highlight how Brown's poems in this volume turn-up "character" in the scratch and scrawl of Brown's intimate hand-written, and –drawn, visual poetry. You can see the handprints of the poet's character, moving poetry itself from the symbolic to the indexical sign. This modest collection of poems, forgotten in all histories and anthologies of important gems of poetry, pushes meaning into a direct connection to the author's hand: a knee-slapping heretical poet's hand. With this squib of an introduction, a mere scribble, that introduces scratch & scrawl, I leave your fingers to trace the flourishing lines that Bob wrote.

"Look Before You Cook," Courtesy of Kaja Marczewska.

"Hommage to Bob Brown," Courtesy of Anna Banana.

Craig Saper

"Roving Hand," Courtesy of Anna Banana.

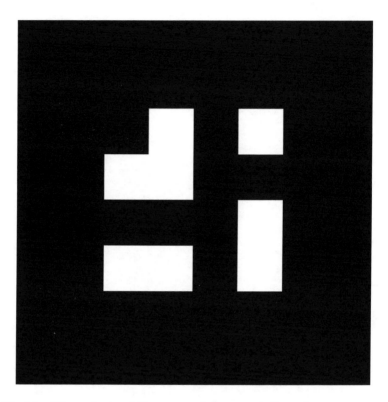

"A Healthy Hieroglyphic," Courtesy of Amaranth Borsuk.

To unlock this hieroglyph, visit the following page and follow the posted instructions: www.betweenpageandscreen.com/bobbrown

Works Cited and Further Reading

Apollinaire, Guillaume. *Calligrammes, Poèmes De La Paix Et De La Guerre* (19131916). Collection Poésie. Paris: Gallimard, 1995 (initially 1918). Print.

Borsuk, Amaranth, and Brad Bouse. *Between Page and Screen.* Los Angeles: Siglio, 2012. Print.

Brown, Bob. *1430-1930.* Paris: Black Sun Press, 1929; a later facsimile edition published with new title as Brown, Bob. *1450-1950.* New York: Jargon Books, 1959. Print.

- - -. *Gems: A Censored Anthology.* Cagnes-sur-Mer, France: Roving Eye Press, 1931; reprinted with an Introduction by Craig Saper by Roving Eye Press, 2014. Print.

- - -. "Letters of Gertrude Stein." *Berkeley: a Journal of Modern Culture*, No. 8 (1951): 1-2, 8. Print.

- - -. *The Readies.* Bad Ems: Roving Eye Press, 1930; reprinted with an Introduction by Craig Saper by Roving Eye Press, 2014. Print.

- - -. *Words.* Paris: Hours Press, 1931; reprinted with an Introduction by Craig Saper by Roving Eye Press, 2014. Print.

Derrida, Jacques. *Paper Machine.* Trans. Rachel Bowlby. Cultural Memory in the Present. Palo Alto, CA: Stanford University Press, 2005. Print.

- - -. "Typewriter Ribbon: Limited Ink (2)," *Without Alibi.* Trans. Peggy Kamuf (Stanford: Stanford University Press, 2002, 71-160. Print.

Goldsmith, Kenneth. *Uncreative Writing.* New York: Columbia University Press, 2011. Print.

Heidegger, Martin. *Parmenides.* Trans. André Schuwer and Richard Rojcewicz. Bloomington, IN: Indiana University Press, 1998. Print.

Higgins, Dick. *Pattern Poetry: Guide to an Unknown Literature.* Albany: State University of New York Press, 1987. Print.

Eburne, Jonathan P. *Surrealism and the Art of Crime.* Ithaca: Cornell University Press, 2008. Print.

McGann, Jerome J. *Black Riders: The Visible Language of Modernism.* Princeton, N.J.: Princeton University Press, 1993. Print.

Ronell, Avital. *The Telephone Book: Technology schizophrenia Electric Speech.* Lincoln:University of Nebraska Press, 1989. Print.

Saper, Craig. *The Amazing Adventures of Robert Carlton Brown: Real-Life Zelig of the Twentieth Century.* (New York: Fordham University Press, 2016).

- - -. *Artificial Mythologies: A Guide to Cultural Invention.* Minneapolis: University of Minnesota Press, 1997. Print.

- - -. *The Bonefolder: An eJournal for the book binder and book artist* 6.1 (2009c).

Stein, Gertrude. *Absolutely Bob Brown, or Bobbed Brown* (unpublished). Printed by Claude Fredericks at The Banyan Press in Pawlet, Vermont, 1955. Gertrude Stein and Alice B. Toklas Collection, Yale Collection of American Literature, Beinecke Rare Book and Manuscript Library.

1450

BOB BROWN

1950

1450 - 1950

BOB BROWN

1450

DEDICATED TO.

ALL MONKS WHO ILLUMINATED
MANUSCRIPTS — ALL EARLY
ORIENTAL ARTISTS — OMAR-
GUTENBERG - CAXTON--
JIMMY-THE-INK — BOCCACCIO-
RABELAIS — SHAKESPEARE-
DEFOE — GOYA — BLAKE-
STERNE - WHITMAN — CRANE-
STEIN — JOYCE — PAGLIACCI-

AND

MYSELF

1950

Without any whirr or splutter writing will be readable at the speed of the day - 1929 - not 1450 ; it will run on forever before the eye without having to be chopped up into columns, pars & etc. ; not risking the wetting of a single finger to turn a clumsy page - on forever in-a-single-line-I-see-1456-invention-movable-type - Gutenberg - Wynkyn - de - Worde - Jimmy-the-Ink-Caxton-though-Chinese-centuries-before - printed - thousand-page-books-on-silk - leaves-furnished-by-local-silk-worms-no-2-leaves-tinted-alike - printing-from-chinty-porcelain - type - same - stuff - that - makes - teacups-and-dreams - - - - - Shakespeare-bending-over-a-work-bench-making - my - language - laboriously - like - a - bellowing-blacksmith-and-turning-out-little - grotesqueries - at-the-forge-all-on-his-own-to-keep-up-his-interest-in-the-job - - - - Stream - of - lusty - steamy-big-fisted-moulders-of-words-Hit-by - - - - Rabelais - Ben - Jonson- Dan- Defoe-Sterne-Walt-Whitman-Gert- Stein-James-Joyce - - - - - - Stephen-Crane's-Black- Riders- Crash-by-hell-bent-for-leather-upper-case-and- LOWER-CASE -together-chanting-valorously-dont-give-a-damn-if-I-do-die-do-die - - - - Print-in-action-at-last-moveable-type-at-full-gallop - - - - - Carl-Sandburg-flashes-through-like-a-dare-devil-cossackism-Cossack - astride-his-mustang-bronco - vocabulary-leaning-far-out-into-the-night-to - pick - up-carefully-placed-phrases-with-his-flashing-teeth - - - - - My-self - I - see - as - mother - father-to-a-new-scoop-for-all-writers-to-come-rhythmical-writers-to-the-eye - - eye-writers - - - - writing-in-an-endless-line-for-my-reading-machine - - - - simple-foolproof-machine-with-printed-tape-like-typewriter-ribbon-running-up-before-readers-eyes-giving-reader-chance-of-his-life-to-see-something-hear-something-feel-something-get-a-mental-bellyful-of-writer-right-before-him-bringing-them-closer-together-now-that-there-is-more-reading-and-writing-going-on-more-moving-reading-and-more-moving-writing. - - - -

MY MOSQUE

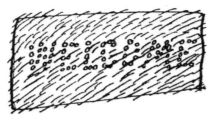

PLEASE WIPE
YOUR MUDDY MIND
BEFORE ENTERING

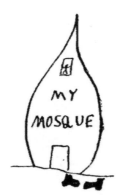

AND LEAVE YOUR
THICK
CEREBRAL SHOES
OUTSIDE

I LIKE LOOKING BACK
AT THE
ILLUMINATED M.S.S. OF

1450
AND FORWARD
TO THE
MORE ILLUMINATING
MOVIE SCRIPTS OF

1950

I LIKE TO SEE
FLY SPECKS
ON YELLOWED PAGES
I LIKE TOO
LEAVING MY OWN ON
NEW ONES

MY FLY SPECK

EYES

EYES

MY GOD†

WHAT EYES !

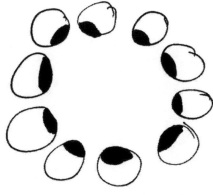

EYES ON THE HALF-SHELL

Tongues
of Flame
of French
of Fire

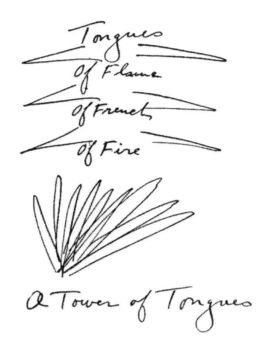

a Tower of Tongues

VIGNETTE

MEN, I LIKE

STANDING UP
WOMEN, TOO

LYING DOWN

DECORATION

Stars in the heavens

Milleflewed tapestries

The Hundred Boys of China

"WILL YOU BE THE APE?"

——— ——— ———

Lines are simple
Plain + straightforward
Why do they always
Net + fret themselves
Into Triangles

△   △   ◁

"WILL YOU BE THE APE?
OH, WILL YOU BE THE APEX
OF MY TRIANGLE?"

THE HE'S HAVE IT

$$\frac{S\frac{HE}{HE}}{HER}$$

THE TRIANGLE

SHE / HER.
HE

HE! HE! HE!

ROMP WITH THE
RHOMBOIDS
TAKE HOME A
⬡ HEXAGON ⬡
TO SURPRISE YOUR
HETAERA

HERE THEY COME
THE BIPEDS

EVERYTHING EQUAL
ALL OVER
ALL EVEN
BALANCED
EQUALLY, INTERNALLY, EXTERNALLY
ETERNALLY
MATED

♪ THERE THEY GO
THE GONADS

V
E
N
U
S

♪

P
E
N
I
S

GODT
GOD BLESS YOU
FOR YOUR SPIRALS

NARROW
GOLDEN LADDERS
WOULD HAVE CARRIED
ALL THE
FOOLS
TO YOU

VIGNETTE
POETS
THEY WRITE, TOO
THE SOFT POEMS
ALWAYS ON THE BED
DIFFERENT FROM THE
WILD ONES.
WHILE STANDING
ON THE HEAD

Japanese print Rain Storm

Rice Growing in a Swamp

The Hairs on Esau

Sanitary tooth brush

and

The whiskers on a Gnat

HAIR-NET

WHISKERS

POMPADOURS

EYE BROWS

TAPETTES

Men and women chase
Each other
Day + night

Monkeys hold
Each other
Eternally
By the tails

INTERLUDE
COLD HEART ♡ HOT POTATO ●
HOT HEART ♥ COLD POTATO ○

PARIS IN PAIRS

||||||||||||||||||||||||||||||||||||

They walk the boulevards all day
Only lying down at night

========================

THE WORLD IS MY
OYSTER

MOUNTAIN OYSTER

PRAIRIE OYSTER

OYSTER OF THE SEA

VINAGRETTE
YOU
WHO ARE REPUTED
TO MAKE.
MOUNTAINS OUT OF
MOLE-HILLS
WHERE ARE YOUR MOUNTAINS?
I CAN'T SEE THEM
OVER YOUR
MOLE-HILLS

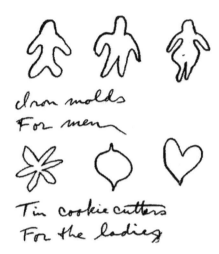

Iron molds
For men

Tin cookie cutters
For the ladies

VIGNETTE

BACK IN THE ARENA
BULL-GORED AND
TOUSLED
BACK IN THE
FREE-FOR-ALL ARENA
BY GOD† NOW
BRING OUT
YOUR PINK POETS

TO MY SON

CRAWL, YOUNG ANT, CRAWL

Yes, young ant
I know the world.
Both hemispheres
I have crawled over,
Leaving tracks
Like this behind

And some crumbs of sugar
To mark the way
CRAWL, YOUNG ANT, CRAWL

00000
only round things
give milk
OO
Breasts
0000
Coconuts
00000
Human heads.

LIFE PROFESSOR COMEDY IT
JAZZ IT WITH YOUR WRIGGLING
MICROSCOPIC MICROBES
PROFESSOR YOUR OVERSHOES
PROFESSOR LIFE PROFESSOR
YOUR JUMPING GERMPLASMS
PROFESSOR YOUR NEAR-SIGHTED
GLASSES LIFE PROFESSOR
ON YOUR GELATINOUS SLIDES
LIFE PROFESSOR STUDYING IT
AT YOUR LEISURE PROFESSOR
YOUR EARMUFFS LIFE PROFESSOR
ALL YOUR GERMS ARE BLOWN
AWAY THROUGH SOFT SAXAPHONE
STRAINS INTO A FANTASTIC
FLOWER GARDEN OF FOAMY
SUDS NEAR-LIFE PROFESSOR

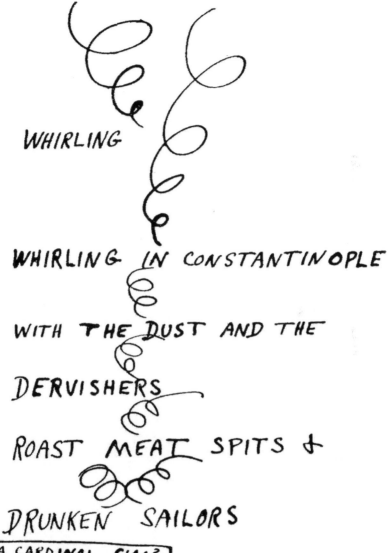

WHIRLING

WHIRLING IN CONSTANTINOPLE

WITH THE DUST AND THE

DERVISHERS

ROAST MEAT SPITS &

DRUNKEN SAILORS

IS IT A CARDINAL SIN?
BLUE-NOSED CARDINALS IN
CUP-LIKE RED CAPS FROM WHICH
PINK-DIMPLED, ANGEL-BOTTOMED
CHORUS GIRLS
DRINK SOAP-SUDSY CHAMPAGNE
FROM BLACK SATURDAY NIGHT
TIL ROSY-DAWNED EARLY MASS
TO SAVE THE SOLES OF THEIR
CARDINAL-THROATED SATIN SLIPPERS

A GIRL
GATHERING ANEMONES
BY A WOODSIDE BROOK

A POET
HAVING HIS POEM READ

A BRIDE
DAINTILY LIFTING THE
BRIDAL SHEET
WITH HER
BIG TOE

A POET
HAVING HIS POEM READ

LADY FINGERS

FINGERS

FINGER LADIES

YOUR LOVELY
LADYLIKE
LADY FINGERS

WHAT WOULD THEY BE
WITHOUT A THUMB
AND A NOSE
TO PUT IT TO

I AM WHIPPED
AROUND THE
WORLD

LIKE A TOP-

PARIS VOCAL
1929

Alo

Pneumatique

Allons

Henri brune blonde

Voila — Monsieur Madame
cinq á sept

Allons

Alo

Finish.

I SPREAD WITH MY JACK KNIFE
GREAT GOBS OF
SUBTLETY ● ● ●
ON THICK SLABS OF
WHOLE WHEAT BREAD ▬ ▬ ▬
AND. SIT ALL DAY
ON COLD DOOR-SILLS
BEGGING FOR
HUNGRY PASSERSBY

HIS MUDDY SHOES
●
HER CRYSTAL MIND
●
SHE COULD NEVER
THINK PAST THEM

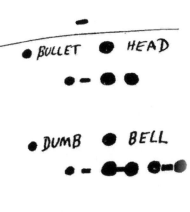

I MUST TELL YOU
DEAR
THAT YOU
THRILL ME

LIKE

LIGHTNING, *Heap*

AND THAT MOST OF MY FUN
HAS BEEN IN FOLLOWING
FLASHES
WITH YOU, DEAR

YOU
Blossoms + rain
Trickles + petals
You ring in my ears

LUFF, LUFF,
THAT'S THE STUFF!

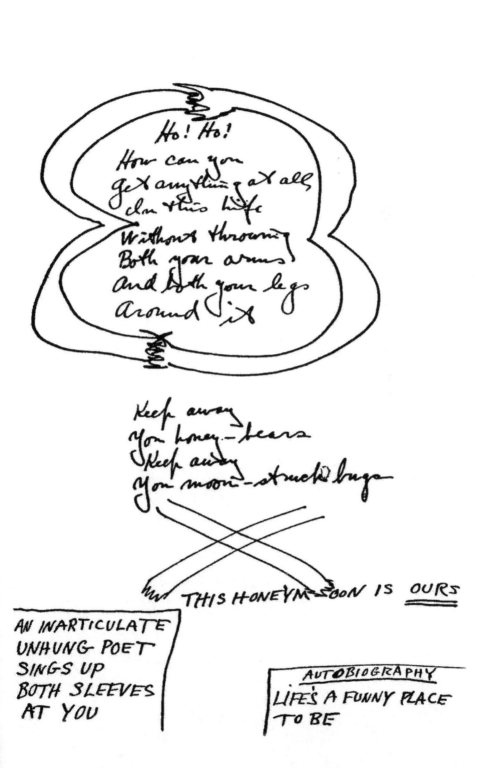

Ho! Ho!
How can you
get anything at all,
In this life
Without throwing
Both your arms
And both your legs
Around it

Keep away
You honey-bears
Keep away
You moon-struck bugs

THIS HONEYMOON IS OURS

AN INARTICULATE
UNHUNG POET
SINGS UP
BOTH SLEEVES
AT YOU

AUTOBIOGRAPHY
LIFE'S A FUNNY PLACE
TO BE

I AM THE LITTLE
WOODEN-FACED PUPPET
WHO SAYS
YES SIR
TO MY PAPA THE VENTRILOQUIST
WHO ONLY HOLDS ME ON HIS KNEE

TO MAKE HIS LIVING

YOU MADE A MISTAKE
MA'AM
I AM NOT THE WHITE-WASHER
I'M THE BOY
WHAT ANSWERS THE BELL
WHEN YOU WANT THE
COLOR
TURNED ON

(5¢) ✦ (5¢) ✦ (5¢)

THROW ME ANOTHER NICKLE
(5¢)

I'LL LEAP FOR IT
SHOOT ME STARS

✦ ✦ ✦

NO MATTER HOW FAST THEY COME
I'LL STOOP FOR 'EM

✦ (5¢) ✦ (5¢) ✦

THERE IS EXULTATION & EXERCISE
EVEN EXHILERATION
IN STOOPING AND
LEAPING FOR
STARRY NICKLES AND
NICKELED STARS

BUSINESS MEN
GREAT GOOFY GOLFERS
COMMERCE
BIG BASEBALL
LIFE
YOU TRY IT &
ALWAYS KEEP A
NICKEL IN YOUR POCKET &
A STIFF UPPER LIP

MY MOUTH
FULL OF KISSES
BURSTS LIKE A
POMEGRANATE
TO YOUR FULL RED
BLOSSOMING
POLLEN
&
PETALS

KISSES
TO
ALL

OFF SET

WORMS~~~~~
DON'T YOU
WORMS ~~~~
KNOW
~~~~~~~~~
THAT BOOKS
AFTER BEING EATEN
~~~~~~~~
MUST BE
DIGESTED ~~~

HIRSUTE
OR
WOMAN'S CROWNING GLORY

I WILL HIDE IN MY HAIR
AND YOU COME FIND ME
FIND ME IN MY FURRY COAT
SEEK ME THROUGH MY
PLUCKED EYEBROWS
TROT AFTER ME
THROUGH MY TOSSING TRESSES
TICKLE THE FUZZ ON MY TUMMY
COME FIND ME
HIDDEN ALLURINGLY
IN HAIR

POLLINAIRE

I	I	I	I
L	L	L	N
P	P	P	T
L	L	L	H
E	E	E	E
V	V	V	H
T	T	T	A
			I
			R

EYES   LASHES

MY DEAR

I PEEP THROUGH YOUR FENCE

I preen
my quills

I always preen my
Pen quills
like a peacock

Before I start to

goose-step with them

WITH A SHAKE +
WITH A SHIVER
I SHED THE LEAVES OF
MY POET-TREE

CUPIDS
HAVE MADE PUBLIC
TOO LONG
THEIR PRIVATE PARTS

THEY HAVE THRUST
THEIR DIMPLED DELIGHTS
TOO PUBLICLY INTO
MY PRIVATE FACE

VIGNETTE
PINK CHEEKS

WOMEN, READING + WEEPING
LONG TEAR TRICKLES
DOWN PALE
MADONNA CHEEKS
ADOWN ARISTOCRATIC
BLUE NOSES
O RABELAIS
SLAP FOR ME
THEIR FLABBY FAT
PINK CHEEKS

THE PEASANT POET'S EARNEST PRAYER TO GOD

GOAT-BEARDED GOD
I PRAY YOU
THAT I MAY BE A
REALLY GREAT WRITER
(NONE OF YOUR GALSWORTHYS, CONRADS
OR WHARTONS)

OH, MY GOD
I WILL NOT MUMBLE AMONG MY WHISKERS

AND THAT I MAY CONTRIBUTE
SOMETHING OF LASTING
VALUE TO LITERATURE
(NOT LIKE BYRON OR BROWNING OR
SHELLEY
YOU UNDERSTAND)

OH, MY GOD
OH, MY GOAT-BEARDED GOD
(MORE LIKE STERNE, STEIN OR WHITMAN
YOU KNOW)

SOMETHING SMART + LIVELY
MORE LIKE A FRENCH MUSTACHE
(MALE OR FEMALE)
WITH A FAINT GOATEE
OH, BEARDED GOD

STEPHEN

BLACK RIDERS
STEPHEN   CRANE
BLACK, BLACK RIDERS
STEPHEN!

AND YOU
WITH ONLY
GOLD TEETH

IN YOUR
WARBLING   MOUTH

THE RACE OF ARTISTS
PAINTER, DIG YOUR FINGERS
INTO THE WHISKERS OF YOUR BRUSH
WRITER, CLIP YOUR WOBBLY KNEES
TOGETHER
OVER YOUR FOUNTAIN PEN'S LUNGS
DRIVE 'EM
PUSH 'EM
DOG 'EM
ANYTHING BUT KILL 'EM
GET UNDER THE WIRE
TO-DAY
FOR   ART'S UNBEATEN GLORY

WONDER
OPENED TWO EYES
ON MY LIFE

(BIG)   &   (ROUND)

WONDER
WILL PUT TWO PENNIES
ON MY LIDS

(TIGHT)   &   (SHUT)

"AMURICA I LUFFU"
BIG NICKEL BIZ
COCA COLA
WRIGLEY
OWL CIGAR
LIFE SAVERS
GULDEN'S. MUSTARD
HIRES
OH, HENRY!

WHEN TRYING TO CATCH THE
WAITER'S EYE
TO GET A
FRESH GLASS OF BEER
I OFTEN THINK OF THE
COY GLANCES
KITTENS CAST AT
MILKMEN

MISSIONARIES

I HAVE THOUGHT

A LOT

ABOUT MISSIONARIES

BEING BOILED IN
BLACK POTS
BY BLACK MEN
AND I HAVE ALWAYS
COME TO THIS CONCLUSION

WHY NOT?

THE AMERICAN EAGLE

10 MILLS – 1 CENT
10 CENTS – 1 DIME
10 DIMES – 1 DOLLAR
10 DOLLARS – 1 EAGLE
10 EAGLES – 1 SCREAM

THE SUM OF RELIGION

1 DEVIL
7 SINS
10 COMMANDMENTS
1 GOD
12 APOSTLES
3 WISE MEN
1 BUTTON
35 COLLECTION

MAN

MOULDED OF
COMMON CLAY BY ANY
RECOGNIZED MAKER
LOOKS BETTER THAN THE
MUD-MOLDED
FAT-BELLIED FORMS OF

SELF-MADE
MEN

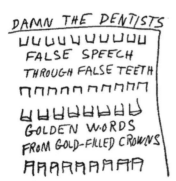

DAMN THE DENTISTS
ᗑᗑᗑᗑᗑᗑᗑᗑᗑᗑ
FALSE SPEECH
THROUGH FALSE TEETH
ᑎᑎᑎᑎᑎ ᑎᑎᑎᑎᑎ
ᗑᗑᗑᗑᗑᗑᗑᗑ
GOLDEN WORDS
FROM GOLD-FILLED CROWNS
ᑎᑎᑎᑎᑎᑎᑎᑎᑎ

PUTTY FACES
PLUMBERS' HELPERS
PEOPLE!
GOD†
HE
   U LP
   M

SKELETONS

SCARE-CROWS

JAPANESE SCARE-CROWS
WITH ALL YOUR
ARTICULATION
YOU CAN ONLY

DANCE
FOR EXPRESSION

DANCE IN SANSCRIT

DANCE IN HEBREW

DANCE IN STATELY ETHIOPIAN

"I WANT! I WANT!"
SHAKE,
BILL BLAKE!
I WANT,
TOO!

WRITE IT RIGHT OFF THE PAG
AND
WRITE
IT
RIGHT
UNTO
PAG-E THE
AGAIN

THERE IS STILL LIFE

An apple σ
a pear σ
a peach σ
And a plum σ
On a hand painted
Peasant plate
Beside a dead fish
And a wicker basket

More Still than Life
Stiller than Death

PAGLIACCI
PAGLIACCI
I HAVE HEARD YOU SING
WITH SPAGHETTI
IN YOUR THROAT
PAGLIACCI
ITS SINGING
AND SPAGHETTI
MOSTLY
ISN'T IT?

SALON - 1929

LANDSCAPE

SHEEP ON THE
SIDE OF A HILL
LOST IN A
SCOTCH MIST

OTHER SHEEP
SALON SHEEP
GAZING INANE AT THE
LANDSCAPE
LOST IN A
MENTAL MIST

DIMINUETTE

O
OSTRICH EGG
O
REGULAR EGG

CAVIAR

[ ] " ⫴ ⟋⟍ ⫴ ◇

Ears

⟋⟍ ⫴ W

Ears of elephants

and mice

Honkeys ears

The kind you can

Take off and

Put on again

¿? ¿? ⫴?

Interrogation points

MIDINETTE
SCREAMS IN THE NIGHT
~~XXXXXX~~
AND A GIRL'S SOFT GIVING
~~XXXXX~~
YELLS IN THE EAR
AND THE LOSS OF HEARING

⟨ ⟨ ☺ ⟩ ⟩

NOSES

⟩⟩ ⫽⟩⟩

MOSES! WHAT NOSES!

⟩ ⫽⟩⟩⟩

SMELLY NOSES
ROMAN, GREEK AND
GRECO-ROMAN

GAYNOSES ⟨⫽⟩⟩
⟨⫽⟩⟩

A NOSEGAY

OF NOSES

LIPS

LIPS CARMINE
CAVERNOUS
CARESSING

LOOPED LIPS

LIPS LOOPED
IN LUPUNARES

THE SEVEN SEAS
ARE MY SEVEN SENSES

THE SEVEN ARTS
MY SEVEN SEAS

⚀ ⚁

COME!
SEVEN!

NICE
VICE
DICE!

ORCHIDS

PERVERSE
PERFUME DRUNKARDS
      BREATHS OF AIR
      FRINGED AND FRILLED
PANTING
WITH PAMPERED PASSION
      FLUSHED AND FULL
      WITH GNOMISH GRACE
O GOD!

TAKE AWAY YOUR

PALLID PANSIES!

LEAD IN
YOUR PALPITATING LAVENDAR
SEX SYMBOLS
HONEY—DRIPPING
FLY-CATCHERS
ENSNARING SIREENS
LET THEM WAVE
THEIR WILD PETALS!
TEAR THEIR RAVISHING HAIR
O GOD!
Watch over your
Blushing roses.

Orchids
With your
Originality

Orchids
With your
Swift, light
Sexual
Strokes

ADAM JOYCE   EVE STEIN

PARIS 1932 AND THE
GOLDEN APPLE OF THE I

I
AM
DO
WILL
MUST
SHAM
WAS
HAM
BE
SHALL
HAVE
HATE
WON'T
DON'T
LOVE
GOD
IIII

ECHO
APPLE LEAVES, EVE
EAVES-DROPPINGS
APPLE SAUCE, LITTLE EVA!

I! I! I!
THE HOLY TRINITY

I HATE
PRIZE FIGHTS

A QUICK SILENT BLOW IN THE
STOCK YARDS   IS SO
MUCH MORE
DEADLY +
SCIENTIFIC

I HAVE JUST COME BACK
FROM A BEAUTIFUL MORNING
PERFUMING THE FLOWERS
I'VE ONLY TIME FOR A BITE OF LUNCH
BEFORE MY AFTERNOON ROUND
WITH THE BEES
JUST THINK WHAT IT MEANS
TO THEM, MY DEAR
I'M TEACHING THEM THE TRUE ART
OF MAKING HONEY

MUSIC & MASONS

MUSIC
THEY WRITE
THIS WAY

NOBODY KNOWS WHY

MASONS
THEY SHAKE HANDS
ABOUT THE SAME

AND NEVER KNOW WHY

SPAWN

I have seen
Man seed.
Through microscopes

Jumping around
like musical notes

Or the Ku Klux Klan
At Karnival

Happier, livelier far
Before birth
Than after

Even more playful than children

DRAWING

DRAWING
BEING OLDEST OF THE
ARTS
IS THE

MOST EXPRESSIVE

YET
WRITING
NEED NOT STAY
SO FAR
BEHIND

THE TAIL OF A RAT
AND A GLITTERING EYE

A WOMAN'S TAIL
AND A PILE OF MONEY

ART

PICTURES ON
TOILET WALLS

BED-BUGS + ANGLE-WORMS
DRAWINGS OF CHILDREN

INNOCENT INCEST GUNS
AN EXHIBITION IN AN

INSANE ASYLUM

DECORATE
o o
o
YOUR PAGES

OLD EGG

○ ○

Autos roll round
On their big
Black
Balloon tires

○ ○

Just as auto salesmen
Roll round
On their big

○ ○

Red
Babboon lips

○ ○

VIGNETTE

■ ■

I CAN WRITE ONLY
FOR THE HIGH-BROWS
AND THE LOW-BROWS

THE GROWN-TOGETHER
BROWS ━━

SEEM TO FROWN AT ME

MUDDY MICHELIN TIRE
TRACK BEFORE THAT
SEA FOOD STORE IN ST. GERMAIN
WIPE IT OFF
IF THOSE FAT SNAILS SEE IT
THEY WILL FLOP RIGHT ON +
RIDE FREE
ARRIVING IN PASSEY
BEFORE THE CITROËN

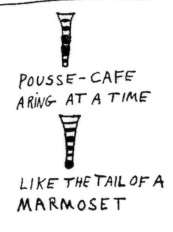

POUSSE-CAFE
A RING AT A TIME

LIKE THE TAIL OF A
MARMOSET

I accept transition's verdict
That words should be
Bro ken up

I only hope the slippery slimy
GLASS-SNAKE ONES
DON'T
CRAWL AWL TOGETHER AGAIN

MERCURY, I'LL CONTINUE
DUSTING THE
/\/\/\
MOUNTAIN TOPS FOR YOU AND
PEGASUS
WITH MY FEATHERED
ACHILLIAN HEELS

MICE TRACKS

ARTISTS
AND I
AND MICE

MAKE TRACKS

ON CANVAS
AND PAPER
AND SAUCERS

WE LEAVE OUR
SIGNATURES

AS DECORATIVELY
AS WE MAY

THE STAFF OF LIFE

LOAF OF BREAD

CROISSANT

VERMICELLI

TAKING ART
IS NOT PAINFUL

IT NEEDS NO

SUGAR-PAINTING

GRAPES

BEARDS

GRAPES + BEARDS

PAN + BACCHUS
WITH MUCH
WIPING OFF OF
MOUSTACHES

LE QUARTIER
THE QUARTER
THE POOR LITTLE
HALF-BAKED
HIND QUARTER
25¢

PROHIBITION

TEARS

TEARS

AN ENCYCLOPEDIA OF TEARS

CUPS

CUPS OF COPIOUS

TEARS

BEERS

BEERS

COPIOUS CUPS OF BEERS

I have written

Out of my heart
I have written

My heart out
It looks now as though
I wear it on my sleeve

That means nothing
It is only a saying
An expression

And there have been
doubting days
When I thought
I couldn't write a
Single line
Blot those all out now
I have written lines + lines
and lines

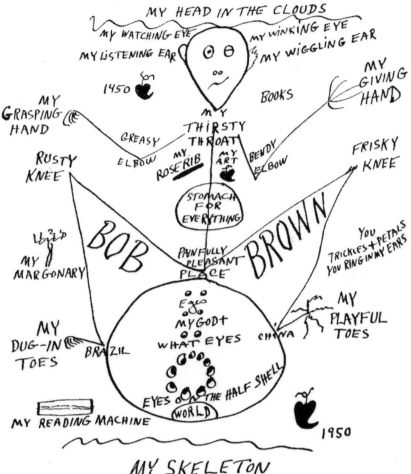

I DON'T DIE!
NO FLIES ON ME!

BOOKS & I ARE BOUND
bound together

B

BOB

BROWN

K

S

our family escutcheon is
intertwined — interwoven
bomb-proof — worm-proof
ETERNAL

Bob Brown's *Books for
Cooks* supplies his famous
catalogs of Culinaria &
Viniana from 37 West
Eighth Street, New York
11, New York.

•   •

Made in the USA
Middletown, DE
11 August 2015